Original title:
The Sea's Silent Journey

Copyright © 2025 Creative Arts Management OÜ
All rights reserved.

Author: Tobias Sterling
ISBN HARDBACK: 978-1-80587-460-7
ISBN PAPERBACK: 978-1-80587-930-5

The Poetry of Still Waters

Bubbles dance beneath the waves,
As fishy friends play silly games.
A rubber ducky drifts on by,
Waving hello with a beak so spry.

The octopus takes a selfie snap,
With a starfish trying to hold a map.
Puffy clouds giggle in the sky,
As waves whisper secrets to the pie-eyed spry.

Uncharted Depths of Solitude

In the deep, where shadows creep,
A sea cucumber is not too cheap.
It haggles with a crab for fun,
While a clam hums under the sun.

Ghostly ships float without a care,
As mermaids brush imaginary hair.
Whales make jokes, then dive away,
While turtles nap through the day.

Flotsam of Forgotten Echoes

Old boots caught in the tide's embrace,
Wondering if they're lost in space.
A bottle cap sings a lonely song,
As seagulls laugh and cruise along.

A jellyfish blushes, what a sight,
With colors that spark joy and fright.
Cranky crabs steal popcorn bites,
While waves tickle them with delights.

Glimpses of Tranquility

Coconuts float like thoughts adrift,
While dolphins wiggle with a gift.
Anemones chuckle at passing boats,
As anchors try to find their coats.

Calm ripples hold a giggling fish,
Who dreams of swimming with a swish.
While sunken treasures giggle low,
Waves splash secrets, soft and slow.

Portraits of Calm in the Chaos

Upon the shore, the waves do dance,
A crab in a tux, oh what a chance!
Seagulls squawk with stories bold,
While fishermen dream of treasures untold.

A fish wears glasses, reading a book,
While mermaids gossip with a sly look.
The lighthouse winks like a cheeky chap,
As boats sail by, creating a flap.

The tides chuckle, rolling in jest,
"Catch me if you can!" becomes their quest.
A snail on a surfboard cuts a dash,
While seahorses marinate in a splash.

Oh, the ocean's antics, playful and bright,
Whales crack jokes while taking flight.
With laughter bubbling on the foam,
Even the starfish feel at home.

Beneath the Waveless Sky

Bubbles pop like confetti cheer,
Octopuses juggle with nets near.
A goldfish sings in a rock and roll band,
While turtles race, oh, isn't it grand?

The dolphins pull pranks, leaping high,
A clam in disguise, don't be shy!
Crabs learn ballet on the ocean floor,
As jellyfish shimmer, oh, what a score!

The sun dips low, the horizon waves,
Fish in tuxedos, gliding like knaves.
Anemones giggle, tickling toes,
As seashells whisper all that they know.

Beneath clear skies, the fun won't end,
With waves of laughter, the ocean bends.
Every creature plays their part,
In this sea of fun, a merry art.

Solitude of the Distant Shore

A crab wears a hat made of foam,
He struts like a king, far from home.
The fish throw a party, all underwater,
While seagulls take selfies, shouting, "Cheddar!"

A starfish dances, three left feet,
The sand thinks it's hip, grooving to the beat.
A whale in a tux just took the floor,
But trips on a mermaid, now he's out the door!

Lullabies of the Depths

A clam sings sweetly, cracks in between,
While octopuses juggle, quite the scene.
Turtles play chess, deep down in the bay,
While jellyfish swing on a bright string ray.

A sea cucumber just told a joke,
But the fish all floated away, barely woke.
Anemones whisper, with tickles and laughs,
As dolphins play tag and draft silly graphs.

Beneath a Sapphire Sky

The sunbeams dance on the waves of blue,
While sea urchins play peekaboo too.
A dolphin with goggles swims up for a peek,
Wearing a smirk, oh what a geek!

A pelican drops by, in search of a snack,
But catches a fish that gives a good whack.
The sardines all giggle, then holler in glee,
As the pelican fumbles and tumbles, poor he!

Time in the Ocean's Hold

A clockfish ticks, but it's always late,
Says time's just a concept, so don't hesitate.
A shrimp with a phone checks his social feed,
While the sea horses chime in, "We planted a seed!"

A whale makes a call, but it's just a big blunder,
He's looking for friends, yet hears only thunder.
The tide laughs at moments that come and they go,
Telling tales of the jelly's new dance show below!

Murmurs of the Ocean's Depths

Bubbles rise like tiny dreams,
Fish tell tales of wild schemes,
The octopus wears a funny hat,
While crabs dance like a chatty brat.

Starfish giggle, wiggling toes,
Anemones dance in vibrant rows,
Sharks do the limbo, oh what a sight,
While gulls imitate them, taking flight.

Veiled Secrets of the Abyss

A clam opens wide, revealing its grin,
A playful dolphin does a spin,
With mermaids laughing, throwing shells,
And seahorses trading silly yells.

Octopuses play peek-a-boo in the dark,
While eels flick tails, adding a spark,
Underwater parties, a riotous scene,
Where laughter bubbles like soda, so keen.

Drifting with the Currents

Sea turtles surf on waves so high,
While jellyfish float, oh my, oh my!
Some fish are gossiping, tales to find,
Others are plotting to leave the grind.

The kelp's a forest, hosting a ball,
Where creatures gather, both big and small,
A whale does a jig, causing waves of cheer,
Life under the waves is a laugh-filled sphere.

Twilight Over Water

As sun dips low, the crabs come out,
In moonlit fun, they twist and shout,
Pirates of the ocean, a silly crew,
With treasure maps that lead to stew.

The waves whisper softly, tickling feet,
While starfish plot, oh what a feat!
With shadows flickering, laughter won't cease,
In the twilight, every fish becomes a tease.

Still Waters Whisper

In the calm, a fish tells jokes,
While a crab tries on a pair of hoax,
The turtles surf on waves of cheer,
Cracking shells with laughter near.

Seagulls squawk like they're on stage,
Flapping feathers with quirky rage,
A conch shell grinning with delight,
As dolphins dance through day and night.

The Unseen Dance of the Currents

Invisible friends twist and twirl,
As seaweed sways, giving it a whirl,
The jellyfish play tag, oh what fun,
While salty breezes toss and run.

A clam protests, "Don't pull my shell!"
As currents giggle and swirl quite well,
They sneak up close to tickle toes,
In this dance where nobody knows.

A Symphony of Sunlit Silence

With sunbeams playing a tune so sweet,
Starfish clap in nonchalant beat,
A whale hums a ballad quite absurd,
While sea cucumbers quietly chirp.

The sand grins wide, as gulls take flight,
Finding shades where crabs hide out of sight,
Seashells shimmer, each one a star,
While seagulls strut like they've come from afar.

The Depths Speak Softly

Down below, a fish gives a wink,
Sharing gossip with the octopus ink,
Mermaids giggle, combing their hair,
As turtles wear party hats with flair.

Coral reefs toss around their tales,
Of underwater ships and odd gales,
The seaweed joins in, swaying with glee,
Saying, "What fun it is to be free!"

The Colors of Ocean Silence

Waves dance in hues of blue,
A little fish lost his shoe.
Jellyfish giggle, oh so bright,
As seashells play hide-and-seek at night.

Crabs scuttle sideways in style,
Winking as they go a mile.
Starfish argue over the best spot,
While the seaweed sings a catchy plot.

A dolphin jumps, says, "Look at me!"
Splashing water, oh, what glee!
Octopus paints with a brush so fine,
Making masterpieces, one at a time.

At dusk, the ocean begins to snore,
As surfboards sleep on sandy shore.
The tides whisper secrets to the moon,
While sea turtles dance to a silly tune.

Beneath the Mysterious Waves

Bubbles giggle, popping loud,
As fish wear hats, oh, so proud.
An octopus juggles shells with flair,
While clams are debating what to wear.

Crabs throwing parties every night,
With tiny disco balls shining bright.
Sea cucumbers in strange parade,
Makin' waves, no plans delayed.

A whale tells jokes, big and bold,
His punchlines famous, stories told.
School of fish burst into song,
Creating a ruckus, all day long.

As moonlight drips upon the swells,
Starfish whisper, casting spells.
Beneath the waves, it's quite a scene,
With laughter flowing, crisp and clean.

An Enigma of Gentle Currents

Gentle ripples tickle toes,
As sea turtles trade funny prose.
A fish plays peek-a-boo with a net,
While the rocks go grumbling, quite upset.

Waves swap stories, full of cheer,
While plankton giggle, come in near.
A mermaid sneezes, causing a splash,
And the seaweed dances, making a dash.

Underwater rocks wear capes of moss,
Ready to rule, they're the boss.
Starfish argue over the best spots,
While clams recount their epic plots.

Currents twist with a mischievous grin,
As dolphins race, they're in it to win.
Mysteries bubble, what will unfold?
The ocean laughs, it's never too old.

Notes from a Silent Cove

In the cove, secrets are kept,
While fish giggle as they leapt.
A crab sings softly, out of tune,
While seagulls dance beneath the moon.

Collecting shells, oh what a chore,
Finding treasure on the floor.
Grass sways like it knows the beat,
While the ocean hums, oh so sweet.

A shy fish whispers to a snail,
"I think I lost my shimmering tail."
Laughter echoes through the waters,
As waves stretch far like endless daughters.

As crickets chirp and stars align,
The cove offers its salty wine.
In this silence, giggles unfold,
With secrets shared, and tales retold.

An Odyssey of the Silent Deep

What swims beneath with such great haste,
Surely they've got a secret taste.
With crabby jokes and fishy puns,
They giggle at the simpletons.

The whale wears glasses, quite the sight,
While squids juggle in the moonlight.
Octopus plays an eight-armed game,
While clownfish jest without a shame.

The jellyfish do the limbo dance,
Underwater in a silly trance.
With every wave, they wink and sway,
To wacky tunes of ocean play.

So if you dive, keep sharp your ear,
For laughter floats through liquid cheer.
The deep is not so grim, it seems,
Just fish with wild and splashing dreams.

Secrets of the Coral Quiet

In coral caves, where shadows dwell,
Lives a shrimp with a snappy shell.
He tells tall tales of his great quests,
While tickling fish with his jesting fest.

A sea turtle wears a silly hat,
And claims he's fastest, imagine that!
With clams that snap and oysters laugh,
They've formed a silly underwater staff.

Anemones dance with floppy grace,
While crabs perform a silly chase.
Fish paint their scales in colors bright,
For an underwater disco night.

So if you roam those quiet lanes,
Be wary of the coral's gains.
For laughter echoes, never shy,
In secrets where the oddballs lie.

Beneath the Surface of Time

Beneath the waves, the clocks unwind,
With fish that laugh and dolphins kind.
They talk of jellybeans and dreams,
And how to win at bubble schemes.

The grouper says he's quite the star,
He plays guitar from near and far.
While seahorses twirl in a tango free,
They're just ocean's quirkiest spree.

An old crab grumbles, grumpy and stout,
Yet cracks a smile when in doubt.
The ocean floor's a comedy club,
With every wave, it's a laughing hub.

So dive into that timeless fun,
Where jokes and giggles never shun.
With every splash, the laughter climbs,
In bubbles bursting with silly rhymes.

Waves of Whimsy

The waves come in, a playful tease,
With frothy jokes riding the breeze.
They wink and splash, they dance and play,
Turning tides to a comical fray.

A dolphin tells of dreams come true,
While a crab walks sideways, just for a view.
The seaweed sways to a merry tune,
As if it knows a quirky boon.

Starfish lounge on sandy beds,
Mumbling secrets in their heads.
They share old tales with fans in tow,
Of mermaids making a fashion show.

So sail along the laughing crests,
Where every wave puts humor to tests.
The ocean's heart, a giggling spree,
Where whimsy whispers, "Come laugh with me!"

Celestial Reflections on Salted Skin

Under the sun, we frolic and play,
Waves giggle back in a foamy ballet.
Seagulls squawk jokes, they think they're so slick,
But their fishy breath gives them quite the kick.

Sandy toes dance to a rhythm quite weird,
Splashing about, we finally cheered.
Whispers of salt, secrets in the tide,
Offers of crab hugs, just hard to abide.

With beach balls bouncing like dreams in the air,
Toward a bucket of crabs that just won't share.
Funny hats bob on heads full of cheer,
Yet miss the seagull that's sneaking so near.

As sunscreen spreads wide, a slippery plight,
We laugh till we cry at our glorious sight.
Shiny and bright, we toast the day's win,
As the stars join the party on our salted skin.

Beneath the Surface's Calm

Bubbles are giggles, laughter unfolds,
A crab winks at fish, oh what a bold!
Floating around in our inflatable throne,
We reign over kelp like it's all our own.

An octopus juggles while giving a wink,
And nudges a starfish to join in the sink.
Fish in a frenzy, a colorful chase,
Playing tag while avoiding a brace.

In this watery circus, we can't take a breath,
As turtles drop beats clean of all death.
We giggle and flail with each twist and turn,
Even dolphins join, showing off how to churn!

With selfies taken, fish flashing their fins,
Our selfies are silly, oh the cringe-worthy grins!
Oh life in blue, such a wild whirl,
Exchanging our laughs with each flip and twirl.

The Stillness Between the Storms

A lull in the chaos, the clouds take a nap,
While jellyfish lounge under a big ol' map.
They wait for the twist of the wind's cheeky grin,
While squids trade tall tales, the giggles begin.

Fish wear sunglasses, so cool in the shade,
While the plankton rave, a silent parade.
Despite ocean's whispers, there's fun to be found,
As crabs play king, on their sandy mound.

But wait! A wave comes, and silly goes serious,
Dolphins dive deep, oh, how it gets eerie!
Yet chaos is fleeting, for smiles return fast,
The calm, oh so cheeky, is never to last!

In stillness, we gather, shenanigans free,
Clapping for whales just to make them agree.
The glee can't be silent, that much is our claim,
As the ocean itself chuckles us into fame.

Horizons of Infinite Blue

A canvas of blue where the ducks love to dive,
As the surfboards float, we feel so alive.
Wishing on waves that our snacks stay intact,
While seaweed gives us the funniest act.

With swim trunks bright, we chase after shells,
Like pirate detectives with tales that compel.
We weave through the tides with jesters at play,
Creating our kingdom from hours to days.

Where seagulls steal fries with a flapping of wings,
And nibble at heroes who wear fancy rings.
They laugh from above at our frantic retreat,
As we chase down our lunch on this sandy elite!

With shades on our faces, we toast to the fate,
Of waves and of fun and the friends who relate.
As the sun dips into an orange-hued hue,
We giggle and wink at horizons of blue.

Whispers of the Tides

Fish in tuxedos swim around,
Crabs hold meetings on the ground.
Octopuses juggle shells today,
While starfish dance their night away.

Jellyfish float like balloons so bright,
Seagulls quack jokes in morning light.
Clams gossip softly, pearls they share,
As turtles strut without a care.

Sunken ships tell tales of yore,
With treasures that they can't ignore.
Barnacles sing their favorite tunes,
While dolphins throw parties under moons.

When waves crash, they give a cheer,
Splashing surfboards linked by beer.
The ocean giggles, takes a dive,
In this watery world, we feel alive.

Beneath the Moonlit Waves

Starfish wish upon the night,
While angelfish take flight.
Sea cucumbers mimic the moon,
Dancing deep to a silly tune.

Turtles wear shades, sunbathing bold,
Crabs sell sunscreen, or so I'm told.
Coral reefs are nightclubs grand,
With plankton lighting the dance floor sand.

Shark spins tales of a fishy plight,
How he lost his lunch to a kite.
The bottom feeders all take bets,
Pretending they're cool with no regrets.

As currents swirl in playful ways,
The ocean laughs through all its bays.
With bubbles bursting all around,
The funny fish can always be found.

Echoes of Distant Shores

Seagulls discuss the local news,
While crabs debate their fancy shoes.
Barrels roll and laughter flows,
In barnacle land where wit just grows.

Shells relay gossip with a crack,
While fish joke that they'll never look back.
Whales hum tunes of a pop star's fame,
Echoes dance, oh what a game!

Dolphins spin and giggle with glee,
Chasing waves, they're wild and free.
A clam claps loud for a plankton show,
As seaweed sways, putting on a glow.

Life's a splash; let's all partake,
In jolly jests that make us shake.
From tides that tease to currents that play,
The ocean's laughter brightens our day.

Embrace of the Deep Blue

In the blue, fish wear a grin,
As bubbles rise and laughter begins.
Eels tell stories of the best catch,
While sea horses knit a peachy batch.

Giant squids craft ink-stained art,
Nautical critics play a part.
Each wave sways to a silly beat,
As crabs break dance on the ocean seat.

With dolphins leaping, carefree and spry,
They challenge boats as they sail by.
One fish dreams of being the star,
Entangled in seaweed, he won't go far.

Every tide brings a twist of fate,
As jellyfish float, swaying straight.
In this realm where fun is supreme,
The deep blue throws the best of dreams.

Shadows of the Nautical Dream

A crab in a tux, quite the strange sight,
Danced on deck, oh what a delight!
The gulls rolled their eyes, quite unimpressed,
While fish swam by in their sparkly vest.

A starfish thinks he's a star on the rise,
Winking at waves with his googly eyes.
Sardines all giggled, just couldn't keep still,
As they swirled and twirled, oh what a thrill!

The octopus flaunts his eight-legged swag,
Planning a party, he's got quite a bag.
But the party's a flop, no one can grip,
With ink everywhere, and no music to skip!

In this watery world, where laughter holds sway,
Creatures share jokes in a humorous way.
So here's to the tides, and their whimsical charms,
Where undersea antics bring joy without harms!

Memories in Ocean Foam

A jellyfish floated, lost in a trance,
Wishing for music, oh what a mischance!
Bubbles would pop, like bubbles of fun,
While dolphins chimed in, racing the sun.

A seahorse pondered, his face in a frown,
Can I wear sneakers, or will I fall down?
He tried on some fins, but they weren't quite right,
Ended up swaying, in sheer sheer delight!

The clams held a meeting, with pearls on their minds,
Sharing their stories, what humor they find!
They snickered at the barnacles, stuck on so tight,
"Better than us! They've no plans, what a plight!"

In the froth and the foam, chuckles do bloom,
As memories dance through the ocean's vast room.
So let's toast to the waves, with a quirky little cheer,
For laughter inside the tides brings the warmest dear!

Serene Passage of the Waters

A whale in a beanie, a sight rare to see,
Singing a tune, 'Come swim along with me!'
His friends in the pod, rolled eyes at the show,
As bubbles burst out, making quite the flow!

The turtles just chuckled, oh what a sight,
They raced through the depths, with all of their might.
"Let's launch a race!" one shouted with glee,
But the jellyfish buzzed, "That's too fast for me!"

A lobster with glasses deemed himself wise,
Claiming he knew, life's secrets and ties.
Yet still he got lost, in a kelp forest maze,
Shouting for help in the most humorous ways!

As waters glide gently, with mirth all around,
Creatures unite, in this laughter profound.
So here's to the journey, in currents that play,
Wit and whimsy afloat, day after delightful day!

A Symphony of the Abyss

In the deep blue, a trumpetfish played,
A jazzy little tune that had all the fish swayed.
They flopped and they floundered, with fins in retreat,
While the sharks jived by, tapping their feet!

A clownfish named Larry, with paintbrush so bold,
Did graffiti on rocks, it was quite uncontrolled!
Doodles and giggles, beneath waves they thrived,
Making art that was quirky, oh how they arrived!

The sea urchins gathered for an awkward dance,
With spikes all a-whirling, they took a wild chance.
But lost in a tangle, oh what a sight,
Rolling away, bursting bursts of delight!

In the depths of the blue, a carnival gleams,
With laughter as music, fulfilled silly dreams.
So here's to the abyss, where joy must confess,
Life's a swim with a giggle, nothing less!

A Journey Beyond Sound

Waves whisper secrets, oh so clear,
Fish hold their breath, what do they hear?
A crab on the shore, he's tap-dancing proud,
While gulls scream at weather, both rowdy and loud.

The wise old turtle, he grins with delight,
Sailing through silence, with shells shining bright.
Jellyfish float by, they wiggle and sway,
A pop song of bubbles, in their own quirky way.

Seagulls debate if it's fish or it's fries,
The ocean's a buffet, beneath sunny skies.
A clam shells a joke, pearls roll in the sand,
While starfish just sit, watching it all unplanned.

A boat on the waves, it's rocking a tune,
With sailors who think they can dance to the moon.
But waves toss them 'round, what a comical sight,
Jumping like dolphins, oh, what pure delight!

Mirage of the Morning Tide

As dawn breaks with giggles, the tide rolls in play,
Crabs don tiny hats, like it's a crab ballet.
The fish wear sunglasses, all cool and aloof,
While more than one clam thinks he's a goof.

The rocks have their gossip, they talk in a hush,
About the big waves that look oh so plush.
Seagulls compose symphonies under the sun,
And clam chowder dreams of being the one!

Driftwood reclines, like it's soaking up rays,
As seaweed flirts lightly, in a sway and a gaze.
The starfish resemble a palm tree gone wild,
While the sea's splendid palette is fresh and so mild.

Oh, how the tide giggles at all that it sees,
As the sun wakes the waves with a tickle and tease.
A fish swims with flair, channels Elvis, the king,
In the wild little world, where nonsense takes wing!

Reflections on a Glassy Sea

The ocean's a mirror, a jokester at play,
Reflecting our dreams, all splashed in cliché.
A dolphin's a mime, flipping wet with a grin,
While seaweed does spirals, as if to begin!

Sandy toes wriggle, on beaches so grand,
They tell silly tales of a watery band.
Crabs march like soldiers, all serious pride,
But trip on their pincers, oh, what a slide!

A buoy drifts by, a jester afloat,
With seaweed for hair, and a barnacle coat.
Fish swim in circles, practicing leaps,
While a lazy old turtle snickers and sleeps.

The rays dance in patterns, a party so bright,
As conch shells play tunes in the warm, circling light.
Oh, laughter echoes through the ocean's vast spree,
In a world where the waves just might set you free!

Navigating the Quiet Depths

In depths where the silence holds secrets untold,
Octopus giggles, so clever and bold.
It paints with its arms, a canvas of dreams,
While fish follow suit, bursting at the seams.

The jellyfish bob like balloons gone astray,
With tentacles waving, they join in the play.
Anemones sway, like a dance in the blue,
Tickling the fishes, what joy they construe!

Crabs gossip loudly, in whispers they plot,
On how to flip burgers, and what goes in stock.
With shells as their shields, they toast by the reef,
To all the wild wonders, beyond all belief.

The seaweed waltzes, like a grand old dame,
While bubbles drift up, whispering a name.
In this quiet of depths, a party unplanned,
The creatures of the deep, together they stand.

The Calm that Follows

When waves take a nap, the gulls look around,
Fish swap their gossip, not making a sound.
Seagulls strut proudly, as if they can dance,
While crabs start a conga, a truly wild chance.

The sun winks down, like it's in on the joke,
Shells wear a grin, thinking life's just a poke.
Sandcastles giggle as they're tickled by toes,
"Watch out!" cries the ocean, "I'm coming for those!"

Chasing Horizon Hues

Colorful fish paint the canvas below,
While dolphins play tag, putting on quite a show.
The sky laughs aloud with its pastel-like jig,
As boats hum their tunes like they just had a swig.

A pirate once shouted, "Ahoy, mateys, cheer!",
But found only jellybeans floating near.
With candy-fish visions and dreams that amaze,
They sail on the waves through a sweet, silly maze.

Echoes of the Ocean's Heart

The tide tells a joke, with a splash and a roar,
As starfish form bands on a sandy dance floor.
Turtles take selfies, all dressed in their shells,
"Just look at this pose! You won't believe the swell!"

With laughter like bubbles, the tide rolls on in,
As a clam holds a mic, ready to begin.
"Let's sing of the barnacles, life's sticky delight,
And how they just cling, never missing a night!"

Whispers of Faraway Shores

The winds have a secret, they giggle and play,
Bringing tales of turtles who think they can sway.
Pelicans' puns bounce on the breeze without care,
While shells gossip wildly, much like a fair.

From reefs that are winking, to islands that prance,
Every wave sneezes, giving fish a quick glance.
The horizon can't help but chuckle and grin,
As it swallows the sun, while dusk begins to spin.

The Calm Between Storms

Clouds gather round, a soft, gray race,
Hiding the sun with an unsmiling face.
But laughter bubbles up like seashells bright,
As crabs do a cha-cha under the moonlight.

Seagulls play poker on a buoy so grand,
While fish hold their breath at a joke so bland.
The winds play the fiddle, the waves hum a tune,
As hermit crabs shuffle to attend the monsoon.

A lighthouse winks with a cheeky glint,
While barnacles gossip, "Is that a hint?"
The calm sneaks in like a mischievous cat,
Paws on wet rocks, with a gentle pat.

But storms roll in with a tickle and tease,
Leaving everyone wondering, "Did someone sneeze?"
Yet between the thunder, there's laughter to find,
A symphony of chaos, the joy of the unwind.

Reflections on Water's Edge

At the water's edge, a mirror does grin,
Reflecting my hat, a comical spin.
Seashells in flip-flops dance 'neath the sun,
While fish in tuxedos are having some fun.

A crab with a camera, snapping away,
Shooting selfies with jellyfish in a ballet.
The tide tickles toes like a playful friend,
While seaweed's mischief has no end.

With each gentle wave, a tickle or poke,
The ocean's dry humor is wrapped in a cloak.
Dolphins are giggling as they jump high,
"Who can make the biggest splash?" they slyly pry.

As I ponder the tides and their curious ways,
A clam flips a coin to decide my stay.
Though boats may rock under rain's soft embrace,
There's laughter in water, a slapstick place.

The Adventure of Calm Waters

In calm waters, a fish reads a map,
With bubbles and giggles, the mermaids clap.
A boat made of pie floats under the sky,
As gulls play the band, and sea turtles fly!

Algae in costumes, they waltz on the floor,
While octopuses juggle from the ocean's core.
The waves whisper jokes through the pebbles and sand,
As starfish applaud with a clap of each hand.

A sea cucumber imitates fashion's flair,
While dolphins regroup for their stand-up affair.
The tide teases fish, "Can you swim any faster?"
While crabs share tales with a hint of disaster.

As dusk rolls in, hues ahoy in the sky,
The antics of oceans are hard to deny.
In the heart of the calm, where laughter does reign,
A round of applause for absurdity's gain.

Tide Pools of Solitude

In tide pools of solitude, life spins a yarn,
Where snails have a tea party, chaos to charm.
A sea urchin who sings at the inchworm's request,
With sea cucumbers bringing their best-dressed.

The clams tell tall tales of their underwater tees,
While anemones blush with the softest of breeze.
A crab wears a top hat to steal the show,
While starfish on stilts take a turn to just go!

Each puddle a stage, where the barnacles cheer,
For star performers, speaking sincere.
With a wink and a nod, they all take a bow,
In pools of reflection, life's funny – somehow.

When the tide rolls in, the audience sighs,
As shells whisper secrets of laughter-filled ties.
In this aquatic comedy, peace takes a stand,
With tide pools of tricks, oh so finely planned.

A Medley of Moonlit Tides

When the moon plays tag with the waves,
Fish wear their best hats and misbehave.
Crabs throw a party on the sandy shore,
While dolphins surf, always wanting more.

Seagulls gossip like they own the place,
While starfish dance with style and grace.
The tides giggle in their watery spree,
As the night sails forth, wild and free.

The Tranquil Call of Distant Waters

A clam once whispered, 'I'm quite the star!'
'Till I met a snail who said, 'Not by far!'
They traded tales of deep-sea dread,
While a jellyfish jabbered, losing its head.

The waves chuckled as they rolled on by,
With seaweed wigs, they came to pry.
Fish wore sunglasses, looking quite proud,
Underwater selfies, they laughed aloud.

Revelations in the Blue Abyss

In the deep there lay a wise old crab,
Who claimed to know how to create a fab.
He told the fish tales of splashing gold,
And all about sailors who got too bold.

But a turtle smirked, 'I've traveled far,
I've seen weird things like a fish with a car!'
Turns out his license was just a bluff,
Now that's a ride we all find tough!

Remnants of Ocean Dreams

Shells recount secrets on the ocean's floor,
Of octopus parties held long before.
Sea urchins giggle, keeping their cool,
While corals plan pranks, oh, what a school!

A whale hums tunes, the latest hit,
While barnacles tap-dance, never to quit.
The ocean's a clown, full of whimsy and cheer,
With laughter echoing, far and near.

Chasing Horizons in Silence

The waves whispered secrets, oh so sly,
A fish in a tuxedo swam right by.
He chuckled at crabs in their moonwalk dance,
While starfish clapped, lost in a trance.

Seagulls debated where best to peck,
As jellyfish boogied, what the heck!
A dolphin declared, with a flip and a spin,
"Join the dance party, let the fun begin!"

Mermaids giggled, their laughter so sweet,
While turtles raced, on tiny webbed feet.
A clam yelled, "This isn't fair play!"
As a clam-shell DJ spun tunes all day.

Then suddenly, a surfboard appeared,
With a group of fish, who happily cheered.
"Catch the waves with us, feel the breeze!"
Crabs in the back sang, "Let's do it with ease!"

Uncharted Waters of Tranquility

In waters so calm, a boat set afloat,
With rubber ducks planning their next coat.
"Let's dress like pirates, and search for gold!"
Said the lone rubber duck, oh so bold.

A crab in a vest took to the stage,
"Don't be shy, come share your rage!"
While sea cucumbers joined with a cheer,
"In uncharted waters, we've nothing to fear!"

Fish in tuxedos made quite the scene,
Chasing the bubbles, so shiny, so clean.
They planned a parade, but oh, what a fuss,
When a seaweed snagged them; "Hey, don't push us!"

"Let's throw a party!" cried a wise old whale,
"Bring snacks and laughter, and let's set sail!"
But the sea cucumbers just rolled their eyes,
"It's a bit too silly, let's paddle and rise!"

Whispers of the Tides

As tides whispered notes, a crab strummed a song,
"Come gather 'round, don't take too long!"
The otters were dancing, tails in the air,
While a wise old clam proclaimed, "Life's unfair!"

A starfish waved hands, totally off beat,
As fish in a line tried to keep on their feet.
"Let's start a conga!" a seagull proposed,
But someone got tangled, and laughter just rose.

With jellyfish floatin' and bubbles afly,
They held their own gala, oh my, oh my!
Grappling and giggling, the sea filled with cheer,
"Who knew aquatic life could bring such a queer?"

And so as the waves rolled, the ocean did sway,
Under the disco moonlight, they danced till the day.
For friendship underwater made life quite a joy,
Even for turtles and that clam, the old boy!

Echoes Beneath the Waves

Beneath the waves, where echoes reside,
A fish with a hat took a wild slide.
"Look at me!" he yelled, "A real ocean star!"
But the sea snail said, "You're not near as bizarre!"

Mussels were rapping, in rhymes oh so bold,
While plankton applauded, as laughter rolled.
A starfish piped up, with a sly little grin,
"Let's play a trick; get the cranky crab in!"

And there high above, seagulls took flight,
Playing peek-a-boo with the anchovies' plight.
With sea cucumbers lounging, all mellow and cool,
"Who's turned my tide pool into a pool?"

Yet with all of the chaos, a joy did remain,
As laughter and bubbles swept through like the rain.
In the heart of the marine, where giggles won the day,
Echoes of laughter danced in the spray.

A Navigator's Desolate Peace

Upon my boat, the compass spins,
The stars above are grinning sins.
I wave to fish, they flip me off,
It seems they know I'm at a loss.

The waves do dance, a mischievous tease,
They slap my face, just like the breeze.
A seagull swoops to steal my snack,
I shout, 'Hey bird! Give that snack back!'

I yell at clouds, they just float by,
With snacks for fish, I hope to fly.
The ocean lies with a playful grin,
'Take a bow, oh, let the chaos begin!'

As I navigate this salty fate,
I find that laughter is first rate.
With splashes big and waves so small,
I'm the captain, yet I stall!

Silk and Foam

Silkier waves do play their part,
While crabs are dancing with a cart.
The dolphins jump, a circus show,
I toss them snacks, they steal my glow.

The foam does tickle at my toes,
I trip and stumble, and everybody knows.
A starfish laughs, 'You're quite the catch!'
As I lose balance and hit a patch.

In a kayak, I thought I'd glide,
But instead, I'm taking a silly ride.
The water splashes, makes me shout,
'Why did I think this was about?'

With each wipeout, I start to cheer,
This ocean's fun, no room for fear.
So here I float, without a care,
In the silly dance of foam and air!

Depths of Heartfelt Whispers

Beneath the waves, the fish converse,
Deciding if my bait's a curse.
I ask them nicely, 'Do I look fine?'
They giggle, 'Sure, but we're by design!'

The octopus laughs, 'What's with the hook?'
I frown and say, 'I'm just a rook!'
They shake their arms, with shaking glee,
'That's a fashion choice, it's true,' said a sea bee.

Shells gossip softly on the sand,
'Is that a human? Look at their hand!'
With seaweed wigs, they prattle and swirl,
I'm just a guest in their quirky world.

With every flip and splash and giggle,
I'm part of this chaotic jiggle.
Down below, we bubble and play,
The fish and I—what do you say?

A Sanctuary of Ocean Hues

In shades of blue, my heart does sway,
Where fishes brush their tales of play.
I paint my dreams in currents wide,
A canvas where my laughs can glide.

A crab in shades of pink does prance,
While jellyfish join in the dance.
'Is this a party?' one clownfish grins,
As I drop my cooler—let the fun begin!

The sun dips low, a slick regime,
While pirates squeak, 'We'll steal your dream!'
I cry, 'No way, just pass me a treat!'
And they roll about, quick on their feet.

In this realm of colors and waves,
I find the joy that always saves.
From playful tides to silly hues,
I've found my peace in this wild cruise!

Silent Calls of the Distant Coast

A crab in a tux, quite the fancy sight,
Scanning the sands, looking left and right.
He lost his way in a tidal race,
Chasing seaweed, not his dinner place.

Seagulls gossip, what a loud affair,
Dropping their snacks without a care.
Fish below swim with giggles and glee,
Trading tales of the lost jellyfish spree.

A clam pops up, wearing a party hat,
Proclaims it's all about a fishy chat.
The ocean's chorus, quite grand and sassy,
Even the starfish can be a bit flashy.

So raise a glass of sea foam delight,
To ocean antics, both day and night.
For in this world of salt and spray,
The laughter's as endless as the waves' play.

Fluid Stories of the Unknown

Bubbles rise up like tiny balloons,
Fish tell their tales in liquid tunes.
Octopus winks with an ink-filled jest,
Drawing maps to the treasure chest!

Crabs in a conga, dancing with pride,
With barnacles stuck, they're well supplied.
Eels in the dark, trying to peek,
Silly as seaweed, squeaking like a cheek.

A dolphin flips, causing such a splash,
While turtles take notes, "That was quite the crash!"
Jellyfish wobble, all floppy and meek,
Stealing the show, yet looking antique.

So gather 'round for a fishy good read,
With tales of the waves and laughter indeed.
For under the surface, fun never dies,
In the tales of the ocean, where humor lies.

Beneath the Waves' Embrace

A sea cucumber, so slow and wise,
Snoozes away while time quickly flies.
"Wake me for lunch, I'm still counting sheep!"
As coral reefs gossip, secrets they keep.

Anemones sway, with a gentle toss,
While clownfish giggle and act like the boss.
"Hey, did you hear? The tide's gone berserk!"
While crabs prepare for their dance-floor work.

Sea turtles mumble, "What is the fuss?"
As waves from the side make a huge big fuss.
With laughter that echoes through fishy halls,
Even the barnacles join in the brawls.

So here's to the life in the watery grey,
Where squishy things wiggle and cavort all day.
Embrace the odd, the hilarity's rife,
In the deep blue, there's laughter for life!

Tracing Stars Through Brine

A starfish stumbles, lost on a quest,
Wants to touch the sky, thinks it's the best.
"Can I borrow a map?" it asks with cheer,
"Waving my arms, I've nothing to fear!"

A sardine swarm, bustling in style,
Whispers to bubbles with a wink and a smile.
"Chasing the moonlight's a daring affair,
But getting caught in nets? That's quite unfair!"

The kelp forest sways, a swing and a sway,
As fish throw a party down the briny way.
"Join us, dear friend, it's a fin-tastic scene!
Just watch for the owl, it's not so serene!"

So toast to the shimmery depths and the skies,
Where every swirl holds a mystery's surprise.
With laughter and joy, it's a watery fête,
In the world of the ocean, come celebrate!

Tranquil Horizons

Waves that dance in silly glee,
Seagulls squawking nonsense free,
Turtles in their turtle suits,
Strut like they're wearing fancy boots.

Fish flip-flop in underwater vows,
Whales are gossiping, oh, the hows!
One just claimed a sunken boat,
Said it's the latest, fancy float.

Clams are hosting a clam bake dance,
While crabs pinch in a funny prance,
Starfish winking with their five eyes,
Schnapping selfies, what a surprise!

On the horizon, a dolphin calls,
"Join the party, the ocean enthralls!"
With a flip and a splash, off it goes,
In search of a seaweed-chips toaster, who knows!

Underwater Reveries

An octopus dreaming of buttered toast,
Jellyfish float like they're playing host,
A whale snores songs of whale-sized dreams,
While fish swim by, plotting silly schemes.

Seashells whisper in hushed tones,
Discussing gossip, lamenting moans,
"Did you see that crab in old jeans?
What a sight, bursting at the seams!"

Anemones blush with cheeky delight,
While a seahorse twirls in sheer fright,
"Did you see that wave? What a ride!
I thought I'd put on a unicorn stride!"

The coral reef is a bustling bar,
With fishy patrons and seaweed stars,
The tide rolls in with its usual flair,
And the party rages without a care!

The Language of the Ocean

Crabs speak in clicks, a secret code,
While boats just float, a curious load,
Seals chuckle, with flippers so wide,
Wrinkled whispers in the ocean's tide.

Anemones giggle, tickled by fish,
Gulping up dreams, they all just wish,
To catch the tide in a giant net,
And host a party they won't forget!

A clam's shy blush, a wink from a ray,
Sign languages taught in a watery play,
The laughter echoes through bubbles of mist,
As every fin gets caught in the twist!

"Who needs land?" a dolphin inquires,
"When the ocean's full of giggles and choirs?"
An underwater world where friends convene,
In a language that's silly, if you know what I mean!

Stories Written in Sand

Footprints meander in sandy tales,
While crabs play tag, leaving flailing trails,
A child builds castles with a frown,
As sneaky waves come tumbling down.

Each grain of sand has secrets to spill,
Like a chatty pelican with time to kill,
"Did you hear about the clam in the bay?
Shimmied too close and got taken away!"

Seagulls squawk out the latest news,
While beach balls bounce, spreading the blues,
Laughter echoes as they roll and play,
In a swirling dance on a bright sunny day.

As twilight falls, they gather 'round,
Sharing tall tales from the ground,
In the sandy stories, laughter blends,
Where every wave brings silly amends.

The Invisible Voyage of Time

Waves tumble in a rhythmic dance,
A fish says, 'Hey, can I have a chance?'
Seagulls squawk with a cheeky flair,
While crabs wear shells as if they're rare.

The clock ticks softly, time's a tease,
But dolphins giggle with playful ease.
A starfish sighs, 'I'm just too flat!'
While turtles roll, asking, 'Where's my hat?'

Currents giggle with secret glee,
As barnacles sing, 'Come party with me!'
How a jellyfish wobbles, oh what a sight!
But all just drift with delight, so light.

In this ocean, laughter is free,
Bubbles rise like they had too much brie.
Tick-tock, who cares? Time's not a chore,
When the waves swirl, it's always a score!

Hidden Whispers in the Deep

Crabs gossip about the latest lore,
'Which fish wore that outfit before?'
Octopuses giggle in their eight-legged way,
As they slip and slide, making bright clay.

'What's that floating? A sock or a glove?'
Starfish wonder, 'Is it lost love?'
They share secrets beneath the blue,
With bubbles popping, oh so true!

The treasure chest shifts in a quirky dance,
While plankton sparkle, longing for a chance.
Clams are singing, 'We are so shy!'
Yet all agree, the eels wave by.

In the depths where the sea turtles roam,
Whispers of laughter feel just like home.
Every ripple holds a story or two,
So dive deep, and you'll catch something new!

Dreams Cradled by the Tide

Shells chatter softly, making their wishes,
As flounders plan their late-night dishes.
They dream of pizzas topped with plankton,
And night-lit surfboards, oh what fun!

A mermaid hums with a giddy grin,
While barnacles cheer, 'Let the games begin!'
Seashells are tossing, cheers all around,
While the seaweed dances, so unbound.

Blowfish puff with a circus flair,
As starry rays float, no worries or care.
A crab becomes king, with a crown made of foam,
In these salty dreams, we all find a home.

The tides bring tales from far and wide,
With silliness tucked in every ride.
Dream on, dreamers, in waves so bright,
Where every splash holds pure delight!

Solitude of the Vast Expanse

Alone on the beach, a sandcastle sighs,
With moats designed to catch seagull cries.
It laughs at the waves that come to rebel,
'You can't wash me away, can't you tell?'

A lonely whale sings the saddest tune,
'Can someone bring snacks? I'm hungry soon!'
Gulls roll their eyes, tell him, 'Check your cart!'
As clams crack jokes, quick wit is their art.

The sun slips low, painting skies in gold,
While jellybeans drift, their stories untold.
Dolphins leap high, with giggles so bright,
While crabs tap dance in the fading light.

In the large expanse, a tale unfolds,
Of solitude mixed with laughter bold.
This vastness is silly, a comedy spree,
Where the ocean and humor dance wild and free!

Horizons that Fade Away

At dawn, the fish wear their best ties,
In a meeting to discuss their skies.
Crabs are gossiping, rolling their eyes,
While dolphins are practicing their high fives.

Seagulls argue over the last crumb,
One takes a dive — oh, what a thrum!
The sandcastles nod to the drum,
As hermit crabs tango, look at them run!

Waves giggle, splashing with glee,
A mermaid's hairdo caught in a tree.
The lighthouse winks, feeling flowery,
While sailors sing — wait, what's that spree?

As the sun sets, the laughs subside,
The fish return from their morning ride.
With tales of salt and a splash of pride,
They all roll home, washed by the tide.

In the Embrace of Blue

Beneath the waves, the octopus hides,
Dressed in colors, oh what confides!
He tickles a crab, the crab just glides,
Together they host a party, no guides!

Starfish dance in a catchy groove,
Their rhythm is odd; they can't really move.
With jellyfish bobbing, what a smooth prove,
The ocean floor shakes — a cool little shoe!

A whale sings low, hits the comical heights,
While seahorses chase their little delights.
Anemones chuckle in silly tights,
The underwater realm is filled with sights!

In shallows, the clams play peek-a-boo,
As splashes and giggles glue the blue.
Stars twinkle brightly, dampened by dew,
Night falls — oh no! What now to undo?

Gentle Waves of Time

The clock ticks slower when the tide's out,
Crabs are on coffee, there's no doubt.
Seashells hold secrets, but they shout,
"You can't find us unless you're stout!"

The fish swap tales of times gone by,
One claims he flew, oh what a lie!
Whales roll laughter, filling the sky,
"Next week," they say, "let's give it a try!"

Starfish count the grains of sand,
Silently judging the beach's band.
"Is that a fish, or just a hand?"
Giggles break out across the strand.

Overhead, the seagulls swoop and swoon,
As tide pools glimmer with a laugh too soon.
With each wave, they hum a funny tune,
Echoing dreams beneath the moon.

Oceanic Dreams Unfurled

Cowabunga! A turtle rides the crest,
Narrating tales of the ocean quest.
"Did you see that?" he says, so blessed,
"A jellybean party; what a jest!"

An eel slips by, playing hide and seek,
Wearing a smile, with a little tweak.
Fish flounder nearby, losing their peak,
"Hey, is it lunch? Let's grab some leek!"

A kraken's throwing a disco bash,
With squids spinning, what a splash!
"Reservations!" shouts a fish with panache,
While crabs do the hustle, quite the clash!

As sunset wraps the world in gold,
The ocean holds stories yet to be told.
With laughter and joy, the tides unfold,
Flat-out delight in the sea so bold!

www.ingramcontent.com/pod-product-compliance
Lightning Source LLC
Chambersburg PA
CBHW060146230426
43661CB00003B/585